Julia Roberts

Julia Holt

Published in association with The Basic Skills Agency

Hodder & Stoughton

A MEMBER OF THE HODDER HEADLINE GROUP

Acknowledgements
Cover: Mitchell Terber at Corbis
Photos: pp iv,16 Bill Davila/Retna; p 3 Alpha; p 7, ©Goldwyn Entertainment/The Ronald
Grant Archive; p10 Touchstone/Disney/The Ronald Grant Archive; pp 19,23 All Action;
p 26 Furniss/Peters/All Action
Every effort has been made to trace copyright holders of material reproduced in this book.
Any rights not acknowledged will be acknowledged in subsequent printings if notice is
given to the publisher.

Orders; please contact Bookpoint Ltd, 39 Milton Park, Abingdon, Oxon OX14 4TD.
Telephone (44) 01235 400414, Fax: (44) 01235 400454. Lines are oprn from 9.00–6.00,
Monday to Saturday, with a 24 hour message answering service.
Emails address: orders@bookpoint.co.uk

British Library Cataloguing in Publication Data
A catalogue record for this title is available from the British Library

ISBN 0 340 80096 8

First published 2001
Impression number   10 9 8 7 6 5 4 3 2 1
Year   2007 2006 2005 2004 2003 2002 2001

Typeset by SX Composing DTP, Rayleigh, Essex
Printed in Great Britain for Hodder & Stoughton Educational, a division of Hodder Headline
Plc, 338 Euston Road, London NW1 3BH by Redwood Books, Trowbridge, Wilts.

Contents

Julia Roberts at the premiere for *The Next Best Thing*.

1 Growing Up

Julia Roberts was an ugly duckling.
An ugly duckling who turned into a swan.
Now she is the pretty women
with the biggest smile.

She was born on 28 October 1967
in the state of Georgia, USA.
She grew up in a small town.
Her mum was the church secretary.
Her dad sold vacuum cleaners.
She has an older brother Eric
and an older sister Lisa.

Julia's parents ran a small acting school.
Martin Luther King was their friend.
His children went
to their acting school.

When Julia was four years old
her parents split up.
Her mum kept the two girls.
They moved to another town.
Her dad stayed at the family home
with Eric.
Julia and Lisa
saw their dad at weekends.
They talked to him
on the phone.

When Julia was ten years old
her dad died of cancer.
No-one had told her
he was ill.
His death had a big effect on the little girl.

Julia and Lisa are still very close.

Julia did not like school
very much.
The other kids laughed at her.
She had thick glasses
and a big mouth.
They gave her a hard time.
But she made up for it later.

As a little girl,
Julia wanted to be a vet.
She loved animals.
She said she could talk to them.
However, at university she
studied journalism.

When she left university
she rushed to New York.
She went to live with her sister, Lisa.
They lived together for
twelve years.
Today they still live in New York.
They have flats next to each other.

At the time Julia didn't have any money.
So she worked in a pizza parlour
and she sold shoes.
She studied acting
but she didn't like the classes.
She also joined
a modelling agency.
But they didn't find her
any work.

2 Her First Break

By 1986 her brother Eric
was a popular film star.
He got Julia
her first small film part.
It was in one of his films
called *Blood Red*.
The film didn't do very well.
But people liked Julia.

Then in 1988
she went for a part in *Mystic Pizza*.
She beat 200 other girls.
Julia played a pizza parlour waitress
who falls in love
with a rich man.
After this film
people started talking
about her in Hollywood.

Julia Roberts with her co-stars, Lili Taylor and Annabeth
Gish, in *Mystic Pizza*.

Just before starting work on her next film
Julia got very sick.
She was feeling better
when they started filming
Steel Magnolias in 1989.
But the director
didn't like her acting
and he said so.

But he soon changed his mind.
Julia was nominated
for an Oscar!

3 Stardom!

Julia was nominated for an Oscar
again the next year.
This time it was for *Pretty Woman*
The film made her a big star.
Her co-star was Richard Gere.

She played a hooker
with a heart of gold.

Suddenly everyone wanted her
in their films.
Journalists and photographers
lay in wait for her outside her flat.
She wasn't used to fame.
She got very thin.
The gossips said
that she had anorexia.
But she kept working.

RICHARD GERE
JULIA ROBERTS

PRETTY

Il s'est offert ses charmes...
elle a volé son cœur.

WOMAN

Pretty Woman made Julia a huge star.

In 1990 she made
another blockbuster.
It was called *Flatliners*.

Flatliners is the story
about a group of
medical students.
They want to find out
what happens when people die.

One of the other stars
in the film
was Kiefer Sutherland.
He and Julia fell in love.
He left his wife and children
to live with Julia.
It was a big scandal.

4 Difficult Times

Kiefer and Julia
got engaged in August 1990.
They planned the wedding
for June the next year.
But Kiefer ran off with a stripper.

Julia was very upset.
She nearly had a
nervous breakdown.
She cancelled the wedding
at the last minute
and ran away to Ireland.

Julia was not happy
but in 1991 she made
two more blockbusters.

The first was called
Sleeping With The Enemy.
The second was called *Hook*.
It was the Peter Pan story.
Julia played Tinkerbell.
Both films made $150 million each.

Then Julia disappeared
for almost two years.
Everybody wanted to know
where the pretty woman had gone.

5   The Comeback

In 1993 she was back
with the thriller
The Pelican Brief.
In the film
two judges are killed
on the same night.
Julia plays a law student.
She thinks she knows the killer.
It puts her life in danger.

The Pelican Brief
was a comeback for Julia.
It was a very successful one.

6 Marriage

Early in 1993
Julia met Lyle Lovett.
He was a Country and Western singer.
He was ten years older than her.

They were married in June.
They had only known each other
for a few weeks.

Julia wore a simple white dress.
She wore no shoes
and no make-up.

The marriage went up and down
but mostly down.
They split up 21 months later.
But they are still
good friends.
They see each other often.

Julia and Lyle are still good friends.

7   A Blockbuster Star

For the next few years
Julia's films
were not great hits.
She wanted
to break away from comedy
but she couldn't.
People talked about
other actresses
being the new Julia Roberts.
The critics called her
a has-been.

But she made
another comeback.

In 1997, Julia Roberts
starred in *Conspiracy Theory*.
Her co-star was Mel Gibson.
He plays a man who thinks
everyone is out to get him.
He tries to get Julia
to believe him.

Mel and Julia had a good time
working together.
They played jokes on each other.
He sent her a gift wrapped
dead rat.
So she wrapped his toilet
in cling film.

Julia and Mel Gibson enjoyed working together in
Conspiracy Theory.

Julia is very close to her mum.
She still lives in Georgia
where she is an estate agent.
She even had
a small non-speaking part
in Julia's next film.
She played a wedding guest
in *My Best Friend's Wedding*.

Julia has a lot of dogs.
One of them even came with her
to make the film.
He stayed in a dog's hotel!

My Best Friend's Wedding
made £22 million
in its first weekend.
Julia liked the bedroom furniture
in the film.
So she bought it
for her house in New Mexico.
This is where she keeps
all her dogs.
She also goes there to rest.

In the summer of 1999
she had two blockbusters.
The first was *Notting Hill*.
Julia played a film star
who falls in love
with a bookseller.

The second was *Runaway Bride*.
For this film she teamed up
with Richard Gere again.
They are a very successful team.
She plays a woman
who dumps men
on their wedding days.
He plays a journalist
who falls in love with her.
But will he get dumped?

8 The Future

Julia is on good terms
with almost all of her
ex-boyfriends and her ex-husband.
She is a kind person.
She often knits things
for her friends and their families.
She has found a way
to deal with her fame.

Her latest boyfriend
is a USA TV star.
His name is Benjamin Bratt.
The gossips say
that they might marry.

Julia is very happy with her new boyfriend, Benjamin Bratt.

These days Julia Roberts
gets $20 million a film.
That's what she got
for *Erin Brockovich*.
Julia plays Erin in the film.
It's the story of a real woman.
She's a single mum
with three children.
A gas company polluted the water.
Erin took them to court.
And she won!

After *Erin Brockovich*
Julia went to Mongolia.
She went there
to make a TV film
about the nomads there.
They keep horses
and live in big tents.

Julia lived with
the Mongolian nomads.
She rode their horses.
She played with their children
and she drank horses milk.
It was more like a holiday
than work.

Julia Roberts is one of the most successful actors in
Hollywood today.

Today Julia has her own
film production company in New York.
It's called Shoelace Productions.
She has her own office
with a big desk.

She has at least two films
in the pipeline.
One is *The Mexican*
with Brad Pitt.
She may also make a film
with Meg Ryan.
It will be called *The Women*.

Julia might run away
from the spotlight sometimes.
But she always comes back
stronger and better.
We have not seen the last of her.